Lightning

by Gail Saunders-Smith

Content Consultant:
Ken Barlow, Chief Meteorologist
KARE-TV, Minneapolis
Member, American Meteorological Society

Pebble Books
an imprint of Capstone Press

Pebble Books

Pebble Books are published by Capstone Press
818 North Willow Street, Mankato, Minnesota 56001
http://www.capstone-press.com

Library of Congress Cataloging-in-Publication Data
Saunders-Smith, Gail.
    Lightning / by Gail Saunders-Smith.
       p. cm.
    Includes bibliographical references and index.
    Summary: Simple text and photographs explain what lightning is and how it forms.
    ISBN 1-56065-779-0
    1. Lightning—Juvenile literature. [1. Lightning.] I. Title.
    QC966.5.S28 1998
    551.56'82—dc21
                               98-5053
                                 CIP
                                 AC

Note to Parents and Teachers

This book describes and illustrates many kinds of lightning, how it forms, and how it travels. The close picture-text matches support early readers in understanding the text. The text offers subtle challenges with compound and complex sentence structures. This book also introduces early readers to expository and content-specific vocabulary. The expository vocabulary is defined in the Words to Know section. Early readers may need assistance in reading some of these words. Readers also may need assistance in using the Table of Contents, Words to Know, Read More, Internet Sites, and Index/Word List sections of the book.

Table of Contents

4

Lightning is a very bright flash of light in the sky. Lightning is made from electricity. Electricity is power. Electricity makes machines and lights work.

Lightning happens during storms. Storm clouds carry rain and pieces of ice. The pieces of ice start moving fast. They stir up electricity in the clouds. The electricity becomes stronger. Then lightning flashes. Lightning is how clouds get rid of electricity.

Lines of lightning are bolts. Lightning bolts are about one inch (2.5 centimeters) around. They can be six to 10 miles (9.7 to 16.1 kilometers) long. Lightning moves at up to 60,000 miles (96,600 kilometers) each second.

10

Chain lightning shoots from a cloud toward the ground. The bolt comes down in a crooked line. Sometimes it breaks into many bolts.

Chain lightning sometimes hits the ground. But the bolt from the cloud only comes down part of the way. It makes another bolt of electricity come up from the ground. The bolt from the ground meets the bolt from the cloud.

14

Lightning does not always shoot toward the ground. Lightning can happen inside a cloud. Lightning also can happen between two clouds.

Lightning is very hot. It makes the air around it hot too. Thunder is the sound of lightning heating the air. Thunder sounds like a crash if the lightning is close.

Sometimes lightning is far away. Then thunder sounds like many booms. The heat from the lightning makes the first sound. Then the sound bounces all around. People hear the sound over and over.

People usually see lightning first. Then they hear thunder. The light and sound really happen at the same time. The light travels faster, and the sound travels slower.

Words to Know

bolt—a line of lightning coming out of a cloud

crash—a sudden, loud noise

crooked—bent

electricity—power that makes machines and lights work

flash—a bright light that happens for a very short time

shoot—to move quickly from one place to another

storm—weather with heavy rain and wind; sometimes storms have lightning and thunder.

thunder—the sound made when lightning heats the air

Read More

Hiscock, Bruce. *The Big Storm.* New York: Atheneum, 1993.

Martin, Terry. *Why Does Lightning Strike?: Questions Children Ask about the Weather.* New York: DK Publishing, 1996.

Simon, Seymore. *Lightning.* New York: Morrow Junior Books,1997.

Internet Sites

Dan's Wild Wild Weather Page
http://www.whnt19.com/kidwx/index.html

Kids' Lightning Information and Safety
http://www.azstarnet.com/anubis/zaphome.htm

Lightning@nationalgeographic.com
http://www.nationalgeographic.com/features/96/lightning/2.html

Index/Word List

Word Count: 280
Early-Intervention Level: 13

Editorial Credits

Lois Wallentine, editor; Timothy Halldin, designer; Michelle L. Norstad, photo researcher

Photo Credits

Dembinsky Photo Associates/H. Binz, cover; Stephen Graham, 1; Mark A. Schneider, 4, 14
Richard Hamilton Smith, 6
Unicorn Stock Photos/Aneal Vohra, 8; Joel Dexter, 10, 12; Betts Anderson, 16; James Fly, 18; D&I Mac Donald, 20

DEMCO